CELEBRATE FREEDOM

Songs, Symbols, and Sayings of the United States

Contents

Scott Foresman

ISBN: 0-328-03674-9

2 3 4 5 6 7 8 9 10 V055 11 10 09 08 07 06 05 04 03 02

Editorial Offices: Glenview, Illinois
• Parsippany, New Jersey • New York, New York

Sales Offices: Parsippany, New Jersey • Duluth, Georgia
• Glenview, Illinois • Coppell, Texas • Ontario, California

www.sfsocialstudies.com

The Star-Spangled Banner

Words by Francis Scott Key

Oh, say! can you see,
by the dawn's early light,
What so proudly we hailed
at the twilight's last gleaming,
Whose broad stripes and bright stars,
through the perilous fight,
O'er the ramparts we watched
were so gallantly streaming?
And the rockets' red glare,
the bombs bursting in air,
Gave proof through the night
that our flag was still there.
Oh, say, does that
Star-Spangled Banner yet wave
O'er the land of the free
and the home of the brave?

America, the Beautiful

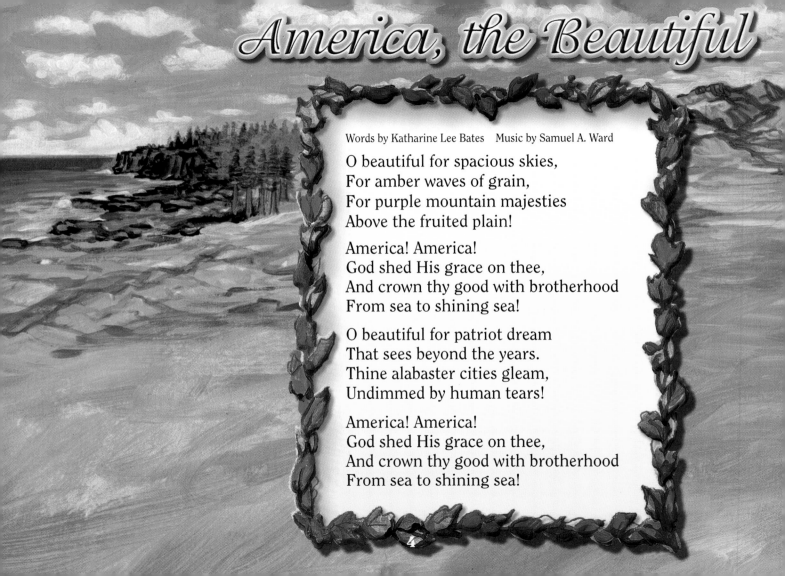

Words by Katharine Lee Bates   Music by Samuel A. Ward

O beautiful for spacious skies,
For amber waves of grain,
For purple mountain majesties
Above the fruited plain!

America! America!
God shed His grace on thee,
And crown thy good with brotherhood
From sea to shining sea!

O beautiful for patriot dream
That sees beyond the years.
Thine alabaster cities gleam,
Undimmed by human tears!

America! America!
God shed His grace on thee,
And crown thy good with brotherhood
From sea to shining sea!

America

Words by Samuel Francis Smith

My country, 'tis of thee,
Sweet land of liberty,
Of thee I sing;
Land where my fathers died,
Land of the Pilgrims' pride,
From ev'ry mountainside
Let freedom ring!

My native country, thee,
Land of the noble free,
Thy name I love;
I love thy rocks and rills,
Thy woods and templed hills;
My heart with rapture thrills
Like that above.

Lift Ev'ry Voice and Sing

Words by James Weldon Johnson
Music by J. Rosamond Johnson

Lift ev'ry voice and sing,
Till earth and heaven ring,
Ring with the harmonies of liberty.
Let our rejoicing rise high as the list'ning skies,
Let it resound loud as the rolling sea.

Sing a song full of the faith that the dark past has taught us;
Sing a song full of the hope that the present has brought us;
Facing the rising sun of our new day begun,
Let us march on till victory is won.

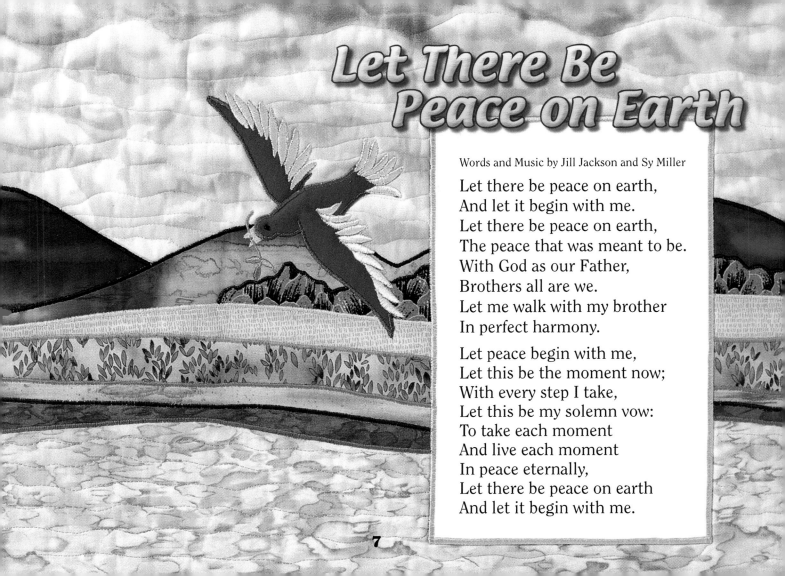

Let There Be Peace on Earth

Words and Music by Jill Jackson and Sy Miller

Let there be peace on earth,
And let it begin with me.
Let there be peace on earth,
The peace that was meant to be.
With God as our Father,
Brothers all are we.
Let me walk with my brother
In perfect harmony.

Let peace begin with me,
Let this be the moment now;
With every step I take,
Let this be my solemn vow:
To take each moment
And live each moment
In peace eternally,
Let there be peace on earth
And let it begin with me.

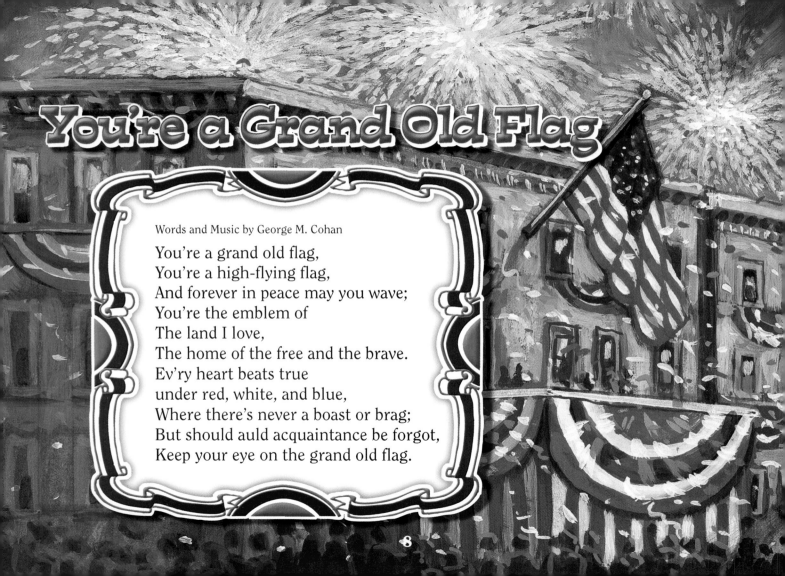

You're a Grand Old Flag

Words and Music by George M. Cohan

You're a grand old flag,
You're a high-flying flag,
And forever in peace may you wave;
You're the emblem of
The land I love,
The home of the free and the brave.
Ev'ry heart beats true
under red, white, and blue,
Where there's never a boast or brag;
But should auld acquaintance be forgot,
Keep your eye on the grand old flag.

Columbia, the Gem of the Ocean

Words and Music by Thomas à Becket

Oh, Columbia, the gem of the ocean,
The home of the brave and the free,
The shrine of each patriot's devotion,
A world offers homage to thee;
Thy mandates make heroes assemble,
When Liberty's form stands in view;
Thy banners make tyranny tremble

When borne by the red, white, and blue,
When borne by the red, white, and blue,
When borne by the red, white, and blue,
Thy banners make tyranny tremble
When borne by the red, white, and blue.

An Early Flag

In the American colonies the first flag flown that looked at all like our present flag was called the Grand Union Flag. It had 13 red and white stripes and a blue field in the upper-left corner.

The 13 red and white stripes represented the 13 colonies.

The blue part of the flag in the upper-left corner was sometimes called the "Union Jack." The red cross represented England. The white cross represented Scotland.

In 1776 the flag was raised on the Liberty Pole near George Washington's headquarters in Massachusetts. On Independence Day, July 4, 1776, it became our unofficial national flag.

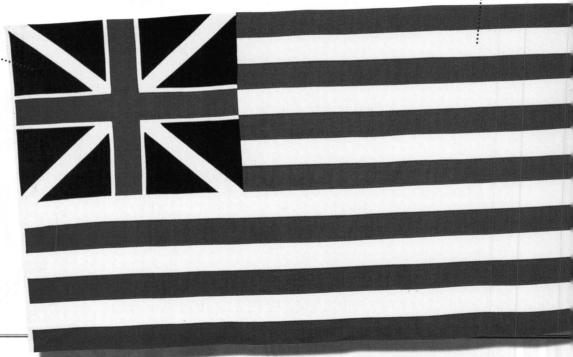

10

The Star-Spangled Banner

The United States of America went to war with Great Britain in 1812. British ships fired bombs at Fort McHenry in Baltimore Harbor. Early one morning, the bombing stopped and the British forces left. A large United States flag flew over the fort.

When Francis Scott Key saw the flag, he knew at once that the Americans had held the fort. The sight inspired him to write a poem, which was later named "The Star-Spangled Banner."

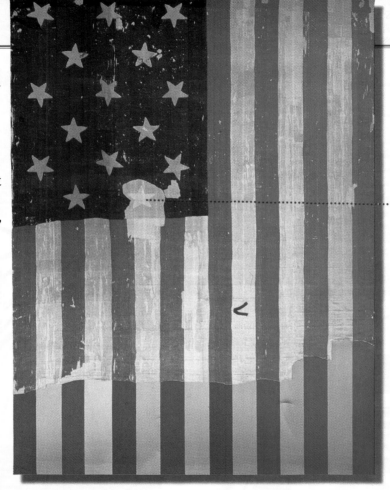

When it was made, The Star-Spangled Banner had 15 stripes and 15 stars.

The Star-Spangled Banner is missing one of its stars. Some people think that it was damaged by a British shot, but others think it was cut out.

Did you know?
People are working to save the flag from decay. You can watch them work at the Smithsonian Institution's National Museum of American History.

History of the Flag

History of the Stars and Stripes

On June 14, 1777, the Continental Congress passed the first Flag Act. It said that the flag would be made up of thirteen alternating red and white stripes and thirteen white stars on a blue field. The stars were to represent a new constellation—a group of new states that were united into one nation.

Stars are a symbol of the heavens. They represent the high goals that were set for the new country.

The flag's colors have special meanings. Red stands for valor, or courage. White stands for purity and hope. Blue stands for justice.

Did you know?

A star is added to the flag on the Fourth of July after a new state joins the Union.

1795–1818

When Kentucky and Vermont joined the Union, two more stars and stripes were added to the flag. This flag, with 15 stars and 15 stripes, inspired "The Star-Spangled Banner."

1818

People in Congress realized that it would be impossible to add new stripes and stars for each new state. They decided to keep 13 stripes to represent the 13 colonies but to add a star for each new state.

1822–1835

In 1831 Captain Stephen Driver had a flag like this, with 24 stars. He called his flag "Old Glory" and flew it on his ship. "Old Glory" has become a nickname for the flag.

1861

During the Civil War, the flag had 34 stars, for all the states, including those in the South.

1912–1959

This flag remained unchanged longer than any earlier flag. It had 48 stars.

1960–present

Our present flag with 50 stars was designed when Hawaii became a state.

Respect for the Flag

The United States flag should be treated in a respectful way. The flag should never touch the ground. It should be kept clean and protected from damage. The blue part of the flag should always be at the top of a hanging flag.

Raise the flag quickly to the top of a flagpole. Lower the flag slowly. When the flag is raised or lowered, face the flag and stand at attention with your right hand over your heart.

Folding the Flag

A properly folded flag is shaped like a triangle, the same shape as the hats that colonial soldiers wore. The blue part of the flag with the stars is on the outside of the folded flag.

Displaying the Flag

Usually, a flag should be displayed outdoors only from sunrise to sunset. If a bright light is shining on it, the flag may be displayed after dark.

The flag should be displayed on all days but especially on these days:

New Year's Day	January 1
Inauguration Day	January 20
Dr. Martin Luther King, Jr.'s Birthday	Third Monday in January
Lincoln's Birthday	February 12
Washington's Birthday	Third Monday in February
Easter Sunday	(variable)
Mother's Day	Second Sunday in May
Armed Forces Day	Third Saturday in May
Memorial Day (half-staff until noon)	The last Monday in May
Flag Day	June 14
Independence Day	July 4
Labor Day	First Monday in September
Constitution Day	September 17
Columbus Day	Second Monday in October
Navy Day	October 27
Veterans Day	November 11
Thanksgiving Day	Fourth Thursday in November
Christmas Day	December 25

Source: Federal Flag Code, PUBLIC LAW 94-344

National Symbols

The motto *E Pluribus Unum* means "out of many, one." It means that we are one nation made of many parts.

The 50 stars represent the 50 states of the United States.

The 13 stripes on the shield stand for the 13 original states.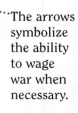

The Presidential Seal

The presidential seal is a symbol of the office of President of the United States. The seal appears on certain messages and documents that the President sends to the United States Congress.

The leaves on the olive branch represent hope for peace.

The arrows symbolize the ability to wage war when necessary.

The Great Seal of the United States

The Founding Fathers thought that a special emblem would show that we are an independent nation and a free people. The Great Seal was approved in 1782.

How is the front of the Great Seal like the Presidential Seal?

The back of the Great Seal shows a pyramid. The pyramid represents strength and permanence.

The eye above the pyramid is the Eye of Providence. The motto means "He (God) has favored our undertakings."

Did you know?
You can see the front and back of the Great Seal on $1 bills.

Symbols on Coins

Images on coins honor important people in history.

Abraham Lincoln
Penny

Franklin D. Roosevelt
Dime

Sacagawea
One Dollar

Thomas Jefferson
Nickel

George Washington
Quarter

John F. Kennedy
Half Dollar

The Bald Eagle

The bald eagle was chosen as the national bird of the United States in 1782.

The members of Congress chose the bald eagle because it symbolized strength, courage, and freedom.

The male eagle is about 36 inches long. It has a wingspan of over 6 feet. The females are larger than the males.

Did you know?

The bald eagle is the only kind of eagle that is found just in North America.

Saguaro Cactus

This giant plant grows in the Sonoran Desert. It has become a symbol of the American Southwest and its wide-open spaces.

The Rose

On October 7, 1986, President Ronald Reagan signed a resolution naming the rose as the "national floral emblem" of the United States.

Pacific Coast Redwoods

The redwood trees, near the coast in California and Oregon, are some of the world's tallest trees. Some of them are more than 94 feet around. Some can live as long as 2,000 years.

American Bison

Also known as buffalo, these animals symbolize the American West and Midwest. In the early 1800s, tens of millions of bison roamed the Great Plains.

National Landmarks

United States Marine Memorial

This statue, which is also called the "Iwo Jima Memorial," shows a famous victory during World War II. It is a symbol of America's gratitude to all who have fought to defend the United States since 1775.

Lincoln Memorial

This memorial symbolizes Lincoln's belief that all people should be free. Lincoln was president during the Civil War.

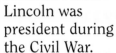

Thomas Jefferson Memorial

This memorial to Thomas Jefferson is one of the landmarks in Washington, D.C. A 19-foot high statue of Jefferson faces the White House.

Mount Rushmore National Memorial

Mount Rushmore is in the Black Hills of South Dakota. The faces of four United States presidents are carved into rock high on the mountain. Each face is 60 feet high. The sculptor, Gutzon Borglum, felt that these presidents represented great themes of American history.

George Washington was the first president. He helped the nation gain independence.

Thomas Jefferson, the third president, encouraged westward expansion of the country.

Theodore Roosevelt, the 26th president, supported conservation of natural resources.

Abraham Lincoln, the 16th president, helped keep the Union together.

At 630 feet high, it is the tallest monument in the United States. Visitors can ride a tram to the top of the Arch.

The Gateway Arch

The Gateway Arch in St. Louis, Missouri, is a symbol of our country's growth to the West.

Did you know?
There are 1,076 stairs, or about 54 flights, to the top of the Arch.

The Arch is 630 feet wide at its base. It is as wide as it is tall.

Civil Rights Memorial

This black stone table tells about the Civil Rights Movement. The memorial is in Montgomery, Alabama.

FDR Memorial

Franklin D. Roosevelt was the 32nd President of the United States. This memorial, in Washington, D.C., has four rooms, one for each of his four terms as president.

Vietnam Veterans Memorial

This monument in Washington, D.C., honors the men and women who served in the war in Vietnam. It consists of the Wall of Names, the Three Servicemen Statue, and the Vietnam Women's Memorial.

Statue of Liberty

The Statue of Liberty is a symbol of freedom. The statue faces New York Harbor and has welcomed people since 1886.

National Buildings

Above the main entrance to the Supreme Court building is the motto "Equal Justice Under Law."

The White House

The White House has been the official home of all United States presidents except George Washington. The original White House was built in 1800.

The Oval Office is the president's workplace. He often meets here with his staff and with diplomats and other heads of government.

The Supreme Court Building

The judicial branch of the government meets in the Supreme Court Building. The Supreme Court interprets the laws and the Constitution of the United States.

The Capitol Building

The United States Congress, the legislative branch of government, meets in the Capitol Building. It is on a hill, called "Capitol Hill," in Washington, D.C. The Capitol has been the home of the House of Representatives and the Senate since 1800.

Did you know?

The Capitol was designed to look like official buildings in ancient Greece and Rome.

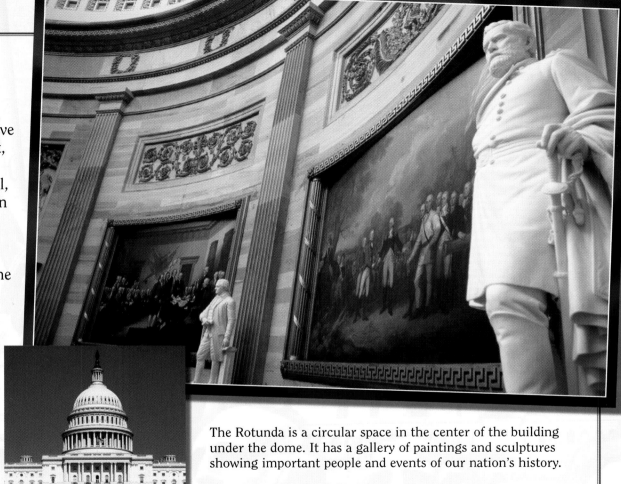

The Rotunda is a circular space in the center of the building under the dome. It has a gallery of paintings and sculptures showing important people and events of our nation's history.

25

Independence Hall

This building in Philadelphia, Pennsylvania, is sometimes called the "birthplace of the United States."

In 1776 the Liberty Bell was rung from the bell tower. It called people to hear the reading of the Declaration of Independence.

Did you know?

Both the Declaration of Independence and the Constitution were signed in Independence Hall.

Mesa Verde Dwellings

About 1,400 years ago, the Ancestral Puebloans, also known as Anasazi, lived in these cliffs in what is now Colorado.

California Missions

At about the time of the Revolutionary War, Spanish priests set up 21 missions in California. The priests taught their religion and language. They also taught crafts and methods of farming.

Monticello

Thomas Jefferson designed and built his home in Charlottesville, Virginia. Monticello has 43 rooms, 13 skylights, and 8 fireplaces. More than 400 kinds of fruits and vegetables were grown in the gardens.

Mount Vernon

Mount Vernon was George Washington's home. It was built on a hill overlooking the Potomac River in Virginia. Mount Vernon includes this mansion and about 15 smaller buildings. Nearly everything Washington's family needed was grown or made at Mount Vernon.

Niagara Falls

The Niagara River forms part of the border between the United States and Canada. Between Lake Erie and Lake Ontario, the river plunges downward at spectacular Niagara Falls.

Did you know?
On March 29, 1848, an ice jam completely stopped the flow of water over Niagara Falls.

Actually, three main waterfalls make up the falls of Niagara. The picture shows the American Falls. The smaller Bridal Veil Falls is next to the American Falls. Horseshoe Falls is on the Canadian side of the border.

The Cave of the Winds is behind the American Falls.

The river deposits rocks at the base of the Falls.

Pacific Coast

Jagged cliffs and beaches with high waves and pounding surf line parts of the Pacific Coast. Five of our states border the Pacific Ocean.

Yellowstone National Park

The oldest national park in the United States, Yellowstone was founded by Congress in 1872 for the preservation of its wonders and the enjoyment of people. The park has about 250 active geysers, more than any other place on Earth.

Florida Everglades

The Everglades in southern Florida is one of the largest wetlands in the world. Its junglelike plant life includes grasses, orchids, and many kinds of trees. It is an ideal environment for many birds, alligators, and turtles.

Badlands National Park

Cliffs, ravines, and many unusual landforms are blended here with the largest mixed grass prairie in the United States. The soils and rocks of this park in South Dakota contain one of the greatest collections of mammal fossils on Earth.

The Pledge of Allegiance

" I pledge allegiance to the Flag of the United States of America, and to the Republic for which it stands, one Nation under God, indivisible, with liberty and justice for all. "

These are the meanings of the words of the Pledge of Allegiance.

I pledge allegiance to the Flag of the United States of America,...............	"I promise to be faithful to my flag and my country,"
and to the Republic for which it stands, ...	"and to the people in the country the flag represents,"
one Nation under God, indivisible, ...	"one country, which cannot be divided, led by God,"
with liberty and justice for all.	"with freedom and equal treatment for everyone."

When you say the Pledge of Allegiance, stand at attention facing the flag and place your right hand over your heart.

Did you know?

The Pledge of Allegiance was written by Francis Bellamy in 1892. It was printed in a student magazine called The Youth's Companion. *That year, students all around the country said the Pledge on Columbus Day. It was a celebration of the 400th anniversary of Columbus's landing.*

The Declaration of Independence

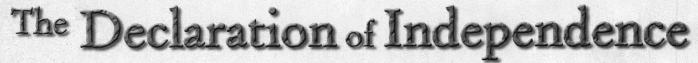

The Declaration of Independence was the first official step that the 13 colonies made toward independence from Britain. Thomas Jefferson wrote this document to tell the world that the American colonies would become an independent nation. The Second Continental Congress approved the Declaration of Independence on July 4, 1776.

" *We hold these truths to be self-evident, that all men are created equal, that they are endowed by their Creator with certain unalienable Rights, that among these are Life, Liberty, and the pursuit of Happiness.* "

> 66 ... it was intended to be an expression of the American mind, and to give to that expression the proper tone and spirit called for ... 99

Thomas Jefferson, explaining in 1825 what he meant the Declaration of Independence to represent.

> 66 We must indeed all hang together, or assuredly we shall all hang separately. 99

Benjamin Franklin (upon signing the Declaration of Independence)

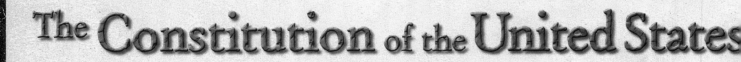

The Constitution of the United States

The Constitution is the framework for our government. The Constitution has three parts—the Preamble, Articles, and Amendments. The Articles describe the three branches of the government. The Amendments are changes to the Constitution. The first ten Amendments are known as the Bill of Rights.

> *We the People of the United States, in Order to form a more perfect Union, establish Justice, insure domestic Tranquility, provide for the common defense, promote the general Welfare, and secure the Blessings of Liberty to ourselves and our Posterity, do ordain and establish this Constitution for the United States of America.*

The Preamble describes the purpose of the Constitution.

We the People

of the United States, in order to form a more perfect Union, establish Justice, insure domestic Tranquility, provide for the common defence, promote the general Welfare, and secure the Blessings of Liberty to ourselves and our Posterity, do ordain and establish this Constitution for the United States of America.

Article I

Section 1. All legislative Powers herein granted shall be vested in a Congress of the United States, which shall consist of a Senate and House of Representatives.

Section 2. The House of Representatives shall be composed of Members chosen every second Year by the People of the several States, and the Electors in each State shall have the Qualifications requisite for Electors of the most numerous Branch of the State Legislature.

[The remainder of this column reproduces the engrossed text of the Constitution of the United States, Article I, Sections 2 through 7.]

> ❝ The Bill of Rights, contained in the first ten amendments to the Constitution, is every American's guarantee of freedom. ❞
>
> *Harry S. Truman*

> ❝ Our Constitution . . . rests upon the good sense and attachment of the people. This basis . . . has not yet been found to fail. ❞
>
> *John Quincy Adams*

Caring

66 The only way to have a friend is to be one. 99

Ralph Waldo Emerson

66 No person was ever honored for what he received. Honor has been the reward for what he gave. 99

Calvin Coolidge

66 We must want for others, not ourselves alone. 99

Eleanor Roosevelt

66 A kind and compassionate act is often its own reward. 99

William J. Bennett

66 How wonderful it is that nobody need wait a single moment before starting to improve the world. 99

Anne Frank

66 We as a people have . . . a purpose today. It is to make kinder the face of the Nation and gentler the face of the world. 99

George Herbert Walker Bush

66 If you will think about what you ought to do for other people, your character will take care of itself. 99

Woodrow Wilson

66 No matter what accomplishment you make, somebody helps you. 99

Althea Gibson

"Teach her above all things to be good: because without that we can neither be valued by others, nor set any value on ourselves. . . ."

Thomas Jefferson, telling his daughter how to care for her younger sister

"From what we get we can make a living; what we give, however, makes a life."

Arthur Ashe

"I look upon the whole world as my fatherland. I look upon true patriotism as the brotherhood of man and the service of all to all."

Helen Keller

"How far you go in life depends on your being tender with the young, compassionate with the aged, sympathetic with the striving, and tolerant of the weak and strong. Because someday in your life you will have been all of these."

George Washington Carver

"The ideals which have lighted my way, and time after time have given me new courage to face life cheerfully, have been Kindness, Beauty, and Truth."

Albert Einstein

Respect

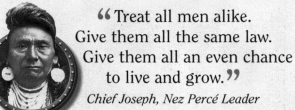

66 Respect for other people's rights leads to peace. 99

Benito Juárez, President of Mexico, 1861–1872

66 Civilization is a method of living, an attitude of respect for all people. 99

Jane Addams

66 The highest result of education is tolerance. 99

Helen Keller

66 I never cared about acceptance as much as I cared about respect. 99

Jackie Robinson

66 Treat all men alike. Give them all the same law. Give them all an even chance to live and grow. 99

Chief Joseph, Nez Percé Leader

66 I must respect the opinions of others even if I disagree with them. 99

Herbert H. Lehman, Governor of New York, 1933–1942, and United States Senator, 1949–1957

66 American civilization will teach [the individual] to respect the rights of others. 99

William Jennings Bryan

66 No race can prosper till it learns that there is as much dignity in tilling a field as in writing a poem. 99

Booker T. Washington

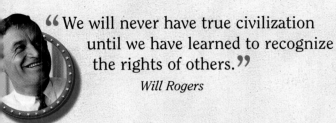

66 We will never have true civilization until we have learned to recognize the rights of others. 99

Will Rogers

66 Men are respectable only as they respect. 99

Ralph Waldo Emerson

66 I look to a day when people will not be judged by the color of their skin, but by the content of their character. 99

Dr. Martin Luther King, Jr.

66 America did not invent human rights. In a very real sense . . . human rights invented America. 99

James Earl (Jimmy) Carter

66 I would like to be known as a person who is concerned about freedom and equality and justice and prosperity for all people. 99

Rosa Parks

66 A civil society demands from each of us goodwill and respect, fair dealing and forgiveness. 99

George W. Bush

66 You can only protect your liberties in this world by protecting the other man's freedom. You can only be free if I am free. 99

Clarence Darrow

Responsibility

" A nation is formed by the willingness of each of us to share in the responsibility for upholding the common good. **"**

Barbara Jordan, United States Congresswoman, 1973–1979

" We must be the authors of the history of our age. **"**

Madeline Albright

" Make your life count, and the world will be a better place because you tried. **"**

Ellison Onizuka, Astronaut

" When we look at our flag and behold it emblazoned with all our rights, we must remember that it is equally a symbol of our duties. **"**

Calvin Coolidge

" The first requisite of a good citizen in this republic of ours is that he should be able and willing to pull his weight. **"**

Theodore Roosevelt

" A nation, as a society, forms a moral person, and every member of it is personally responsible for his society. **"**

Thomas Jefferson

66 Responsibility is the price
of greatness. 99

Winston Churchill

66 What happens to the country,
to the world, depends on what we do
with what others have left us. 99

Robert Kennedy

66 You will find men who want
to be carried on the shoulders of others,
who think that the world owes them a living.
They don't seem to see that we must
all lift together and pull together. 99

Henry Ford

66 Because you live in a democracy,
you also take on responsibility for your society
and your community. 99

Ann Richards, Governor of Texas, 1991–1995

66 To make our way, we must . . .
gear ourselves to
work hard all the way. 99

Ralph Bunche, American Statesman

66 And so, my fellow Americans:
ask not what your country can do for you.
Ask what you can do for your country. 99

John F. Kennedy

Fairness

"This country will not be a permanently good place for any of us to live in unless we make it a reasonably good place for all of us to live in."

Theodore Roosevelt

"Every segment of our population and every individual has a right to expect from his government a fair deal."

Harry S. Truman

"We must live together as brothers or perish together as fools."

Dr. Martin Luther King, Jr.

"The earth is the mother of all people, and all people should have equal rights upon it."

Chief Joseph, Nez Percé Leader

"Justice is indiscriminately due to all, without regard to numbers, wealth, or rank."

John Jay, first Chief Justice of the Supreme Court

"Though force can protect in emergency, only justice, fairness, consideration, and cooperation can finally lead men to the dawn of eternal peace."

Dwight D. Eisenhower

"Fairness is an across-the-board requirement for all our interactions with each other. . . . Fairness treats everybody the same."

Barbara Jordan

"The rights of every man are diminished when the rights of one man are threatened."

John F. Kennedy

"We cannot seek achievement for ourselves and forget about progress and prosperity for our community. . . . Our ambitions must be broad enough to include the needs of others, for their sakes and for our own."

César Chávez

"From the earliest history of our country, woman has shown equal devotion with man to the cause of freedom. . . . We ask justice, we ask equality, we ask that all the civil and political rights that belong to citizens of the United States be guaranteed to us and our daughters forever."

Elizabeth Cady Stanton

"The rights of men are: liberty, safety, private property, and equality."

Simón Bolívar, South American Independence Leader

"Justice is the crowning glory of the virtues."

Marcus Tullius Cicero,
Roman Statesman, 106 B.C.–43 B.C.

Honesty

66 Honesty in States, as well as Individuals, will ever be found the soundest policy. 99

George Washington

66 Every truth we see is one to give the world, not to keep to ourselves alone. 99

Elizabeth Cady Stanton

66 I would give no thought of what the world might say of me; I could only transmit to posterity the reputation of an honest man. 99

Sam Houston

66 The world is moved along, not by the mighty shoves of its heroes, but also by the . . . tiny pushes of each honest worker. 99

Helen Keller

66 Truth is always exciting. Speak it, then. Life is dull without it. 99

Pearl S. Buck, Writer

66 An honest man will receive neither money nor praise, that is not his due. 99

Benjamin Franklin

66 The greatest homage we can pay to truth, is to use it. 99

James Russell Lowell

"The life of the nation is secure only while the nation is honest, truthful, and virtuous."
Frederick Douglass

"I believe that unarmed truth and unconditional love will have the final word in reality."
Dr. Martin Luther King, Jr.

"Truth is the property of no individual but is the treasure of all men."
Ralph Waldo Emerson

"May none but honest and wise men ever rule beneath this roof."
John Adams,
writing about the White House

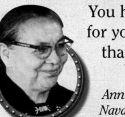

"You have to be honest with people. You have to have great respect for yourself. If you see something that is not right, you must do something about it."
Annie Dodge Wauneka,
Navajo Health Educator

"The one thing I want to leave my children is an honorable name."
Theodore Roosevelt

"To make your children capable of honesty is the beginning of education."
John Ruskin,
British Writer and Artist

Courage

66 Courage is the virtue on which all the other virtues mount. 99

Clare Boothe Luce

66 America at its best is also courageous. We must show courage in a time of blessing, by confronting problems instead of passing them on to future generations. 99

George W. Bush

66 The man who rises once again is greater than the one who has never fallen. 99

Conception Arenal,
Spanish Writer

66 Standing for right when it is unpopular is a true test of moral character. 99

Margaret Chase Smith,
United States Congresswoman, 1940–1948, and
United States Senator, 1948–1973

66 You gain strength, courage, and confidence by every experience in which you really stop to look fear directly in the face. You must do the thing which you think you cannot do. 99

Eleanor Roosevelt

66 This will remain the land of the free only so long as it is the home of the brave. 99

Elmer Davis

66 Our challenges ought not defeat us; rather, they should drive us. 99

Dr. David Satcher,
United States Surgeon General, 1998–2002

66 If you doubt you can accomplish something, then you can't accomplish it.
You have to have confidence in your ability, and then be tough enough to follow through. 99

Rosalyn Carter

66 Courage is reckoned the greatest of all virtues; because, unless a man has that virtue, he has no security for preserving any other. 99

Samuel Johnson

66 Freedom lies in being bold. 99

Robert Frost

66 Without courage, we cannot practice any other virtue with consistency.
We can't be kind, true, merciful, generous, or honest. 99

Dr. Maya Angelou

66 Courage is the price that life exacts for granting peace with yourself. 99

· *Amelia Earhart*

Credits